Greater Than a T(

Reviews from Readers

I think the series is wonderful and beneficial for tourists to get information before visiting the city.

-Seckin Zumbul, Izmir Turkey

I am a world traveler who has read many trip guides but this one really made a difference for me. I would call it a heartfelt creation of a local guide expert instead of just a guide.

-Susy, Isla Holbox, Mexico

New to the area like me, this is a must have!

-Joe, Bloomington, USA

This is a good series that gets down to it when looking for things to do at your destination without having to read a novel for just a few ideas.

-Rachel, Monterey, USA

Good information to have to plan my trip to this destination.

-Pennie Farrell, Mexico

Great ideas for a port day.

-Mary Martin USA

Tanja Andric

Aptly titled, you won't just be a tourist after reading this book. You'll be greater than a tourist!

-Alan Warner, Grand Rapids, USA

Thank you for a fantastic book.

-Don, Philadelphia, USA

Even though I only have three days to spend in San Miguel in an upcoming visit, I will use the author's suggestions to guide some of my time there. An easy read - with chapters named to guide me in directions I want to go.

-Robert Catapano, USA

Great insights from a local perspective! Useful information and a very good value!

-Sarah, USA

This series provides an in-depth experience through the eyes of a local. Reading these series will help you to travel the city in with confidence and it'll make your journey a unique one.

-Andrew Teoh, Ipoh, Malaysia

GREATER THAN A TOURIST – AYIA NAPA CYPRUS

50 Travel Tips from a Local

Tanja Andric

Tanja Andric

Cover designed by:
Cover Image: https://pixabay.com/en/path-coppice-copse-forest-trees-3171743/

Greater Than a Tourist
Visit our website at www.GreaterThanaTourist.com

Lock Haven, PA
ISBN: 9781980921417

>TOURIST

50 TRAVEL TIPS FROM A LOCAL

Tanja Andric

BOOK DESCRIPTION

Are you excited about planning your next trip?

Do you want to try something new?

Would you like some guidance from a local?

If you answered yes to any of these questions, then this Greater Than a Tourist book is for you.

Greater Than a Tourist- Ayia Napa Cyprus by Tanja Andric offers the inside scoop on Ayia Napa. Most travel books tell you how to travel like a tourist. Although there is nothing wrong with that, as part of the Greater Than a Tourist series, this book will give you travel tips from someone who has lived at your next travel destination.

In these pages, you will discover advice that will help you throughout your stay. This book will not tell you exact addresses or store hours but instead will give you excitement and knowledge from a local that you may not find in other smaller print travel books.

Travel like a local. Slow down, stay in one place, and get to know the people and the culture. By the time you finish this book, you will be eager and prepared to travel to your next destination.

Tanja Andric

TABLE OF CONTENTS

14. PARKO PALIATSO LUNA PARK
15. SLING SHOT
16. ZORBAS BAKERY
17. BEDROCK INN
18. AYIA THEKLA CHAPEL
19. SING LIKE NOBODY IS LISTENING
20. VISIT PROTARAS
21. MAGIC DANCING WATERS
22. KONNOS BAY
23. FIG TREE BAY
24. LOS BANDIDOS
25. PLAY TAVLI
26. CYPRUS MEZE
27. BRANDY SOUR
28. UV PAINT PARTY
29. FAMOUS LOCAL SPIRITS
30. HALLOUMI
31. ESCAPE ROOMS EXPERIENCE
32. TIE THE KNOT!
33. GHOST TOWN FAMAGUSTA
34. KAMARA TOU KORAKA
35. WALKING TOUR
36. EXPLORE THE VILLAGE ON WHEELS
37. RIVER REGGAE PUB
38. SHIPWRECK DIVING
39. FINE DINING

DEDICATION

This book is dedicated to my family, for all the love, understanding and support throughout my life.

Tanja Andric

ABOUT THE AUTHOR

Tanja Andric is a mother of two, a writer, cat lover and very passionate about traveling. She is located in Belgrade, Serbia, but left her heart in Cyprus long time ago, where she lived and worked, and got addicted to azure and emerald beaches, constant sunshine, and delicious food.

This guidebook is her inside scoop, so explore it and enjoy it!

Tanja Andric

HOW TO USE THIS BOOK

The Greater Than a Tourist book series was written by someone who has lived in an area for over three months. The goal of this book is to help travelers either dream or experience different locations by providing opinions from a local. The author has made suggestions based on their own experiences. Please do your own research before traveling to the area in case the suggested places are unavailable.

Tanja Andric

FROM THE PUBLISHER

Traveling can be one of the most important parts of a person's life. The anticipation and memories that you have are some of the best. As a publisher of the Greater Than a Tourist book series, as well as the popular 50 Things to Know book series, we strive to help you learn about new places, spark your imagination, and inspire you. Wherever you are and whatever you do I wish you safe, fun, and inspiring travel.

Lisa Rusczyk Ed. D.
CZYK Publishing

Tanja Andric

OUR STORY

Traveling is a passion of the "Greater than a Tourist" series creator. Lisa studied abroad in college, and for their honeymoon Lisa and her husband toured Europe. During her travels to Malta, an older man tried to give her some advice based on his own experience living on the island since he was a young boy. She was not sure if she should talk to the stranger but was interested in his advice. When traveling to some places she was wary to talk to locals because she was afraid that they weren't being genuine. Through her travels, Lisa learned how much locals had to share with tourists. Lisa created the "Greater Than a Tourist" book series to help connect people with locals. A topic that locals are very passionate about sharing.

Tanja Andric

WELCOME TO
> TOURIST

Tanja Andric

INTRODUCTION

Don't tell me how educated you are, tell me how much you travelled.

Mohamed

In the following pages you will find 50 things that I have personally done and places I have visited.

Ayia Napa is a wonderful and vibrant village, equally loved by party animals and retired senior couples. The reason is simple: it has so much to offer, different fun for everyone.

Beaches are amazingly beautiful, perfect for *#nofilter* Instagram posts: long, sandy and romantic or rough and rocky, you will find the right one to your taste. Nissi beach is in the top 3 of the most Instagrammed beaches in the world!

A beautiful and quiet Orthodox monastery is set in the heart of the busy Ayia Napa Square.

Charming taverns and fine dining restaurants, loud karaoke pubs, whatever your heart desires, Ayia Napa has it all!

Tanja Andric

With the summer months it is becoming increasingly fuller of tourists, but still remains one of the top summer destinations and interesting places in Europe.

My advice is to visit without delay and see for yourself what this guidebook is about and enjoy to the fullest.

1. INHALE!

The moment you land in Cyprus, and leave the building of Larnaca Airport, inhale that air. Feel in your nostrils the warm mixture of salt and coconut sunscreen. Bear in mind that during July and August humidity is very high, so don't be surprised if your hair just looses or you start sweating uncontrollably. Nobody cares, trust me!

2. NISSI BEACH

Nissi beach is a must! A stunning beach with crystal clear waters and white powdery sand, stretching 500m (1640Ft), is one of the island's most visited beaches each year. This is a legendary place where many world class parties were held (MTV Base Beach Party, Geordie Shore Ayia Napa party, etc). Every summer, the local Nissi Bay Beach Bar is hosting foam parties twice a week. Enjoy cool refreshments, linger under the sun, mingle with the beautiful people who flock here, and take as many photos as you can, and don't forget: #nofilter

3. MAKRONISSOS BEACH

A beautiful, quiet beach, close to Waterworld, one of the first beaches you'll see when you enter Ayia Napa on your way from the airport. It is made up of several smaller beaches, all interlinked with pathways. The emerald water is so clear that even on bigger depths you can see rocks and tiny fish. Watersports are everywhere, it is very relaxing and peaceful, first choice for families with kids and those who are fond of reading books on the beach. However, don't see Makronissos as the lazy beach for senior citizens - MTV hosted some excellent parties here!

4. WATERWORLD

Sheer fun! Fun for toddlers, teens, families, thrill-seekers, Instagram-junkies, everyone! WaterWorld Waterpark is ancient Greek themed waterpark and is one of the largest themed waterparks in Europe. It has numerous rides and attractions, lounge areas, restaurant, and my all-time favorite: Adults only pool with jets and bubble benches. Before paying the full price of the entrance, look for discount flyers stacked in almost every hotel and apartment building.

5. KAVO GREKO/CAPE GREKO

Kavo Greko /Cape Greko is a protected National Forest Park that is home to serious number of endemic herbal species. It is located halfway between Ayia Napa and Protaras. It represents a good starting point for hikers, as there you can find great nature hiking trails and stunning nature monuments (Kamara Tou Koraka and Love brigde). Its rough scenery and turquoise water will definitely take your breath away. Go dive, explore caves, cliff jump, hike or simply take a few shots and rest in the sun. Don't forget to visit the lovely small white chapel dedicated to Agioi Anargyroi (the two brothers, Saints Cosmas and Damianos who were doctors) which is a very popular spot for taking photos.

6. SEA CAVES

There are many sea caves along the coastline from Agia Napa to Cape Greko National Park. People flock here to snorkel and locals come here before dawn to fish. There are spots of deep water amongst the rocks where daredevils engage in cliff jumping. The water is wonderfully clear and it's simply tempting you to jump in.

7. THALASSA MUSEUM

Really great place to spend a couple of hours in and learn something about marine life of Cyprus, and see fish and sea mammals, corals, shells and fossils - some dating back 130 million years ago! Also, there is a replica of a famous Greek trading ship Keryneia II that sank off the coast of Keryneia around 300 BC! It is a modern, interactive museum, but from my point of view needs a serious restauration, as you could see that some stuffed animals were rotting away.

8. THE SQUARE

I really don't know what to write here. The Square is simply – the Square! It's the town's bellybutton. It's the most popular meeting point. It is the starting point for bar crawlers. It is where night vibes start spreading. It is the place where all national celebrations begin and end. It's definitely the place you visit last before heading to the cab or bus on your way back to the airport.

9. AYIA NAPA MONASTERY

This is a, believe it or not, medieval monastery, built in 16th century. It is located in the heart of Ayia Napa, in the middle of the Square! The Monastery is dedicated to Our Lady of the Forest. Can you imagine the thick forest instead of today's Ayia Napa? The village name itself means "thick forest". According to the local legend, a hunter found a cave which has been made into church, and inside the church, he found an icon of the Virgin Mary. His dog saw the glowing light of an icon and began to bark.

The monastery offers a haven of tranquility, and in hot summer days, the giant sycamore tree will provide you with shade. Unlike most churches and monasteries in Cyprus, this one has survived the Ottoman rule. In the peak of the day, it seems like you are muted from the outer world in this beautiful and tranquil place. It is impossible not to enjoy the silence, sometimes interrupted by birds chirping.

Please, follow the dress code suitable for Holy Grounds, when entering this unique Monastery. Entrance is free, so say a prayer, light a few candles or simply hide away from the heat. And of course, don't forget to take photos!

10. SCULPTURE PARK

This is an exquisite way to show your friends that you are also an art loving person, and that Ayia Napa is not all about clubs, booze and beaches. This lovely site is located just outside the village, on the way to Protaras. It is an open air museum with works of different artists which is growing every year with some new pieces being added to the existing collection. It has it all: sculptures, rocky landscape, sea view, no entrance fee. All you need is a pair of comfy shoes and a camera, of course.

11. MAKRONISSOS TOMBS

Taste the dirt and strong sun on your face while you explore nineteen tombs from Roman and Hellenistic period, proving yourself better than Lara

Croft. This is very exciting tip, because those tombs were excavated in the late 1980's, and they date back to 2400 BC! They are located very close to Makronissos beach, and after exciting excursion, it will take you ten minutes to toss your clothes on the beach towel and dip into the water to chill!

12. AYIA NAPA SEA MONSTER

Surrounded by the sea, with all those rocks, cliffs, shipwrecks, rich marine life, it would really be unthinkable for Cyprus not to have a personal sea monster. For a certain reason that particular monster decided to settle close to the Ayia Napa coast. The creature is giving headache to fishermen for decades, tearing their nets apart, but not harming anyone ever. That's why the locals named it "To Filiko Teras" – meaning, The Friendly Monster. It is mostly reported to be seen in the Cape Greko area, but there was never any evidence, photo, footage, nothing. The hope of spotting the Ayia Napa Sea Monster remains a highlight for many tourists on boating day-trips. Maybe, you'll be the lucky one?

Tanja Andric

13. BLACK PEARL PIRATE BOAT

Have you seen Pirates of the Caribbean? Well here's Pirates of the Mediterranean*. Beautiful, black replica of the most popular pirate boat in the recent movie history is sailing your way to pick you up and take you to the best themed cruise in Cyprus. Captain Jack Sparrow and his pirates will provide family fun during day. It will take you along the East coast of Cyprus where you can enjoy the view of Ayia Napa Sea Caves, Cavo Greko, Konnos Bay and the beautiful Fig Tree Bay in Protaras. Walk the plank and have fun taking part in the pirate show. There is a treasure hunt for kids, and of course, buffet lunch.

*Official line of the Black Pearl Pirate Boat

14. PARKO PALIATSO LUNA PARK

The biggest entertainment park in Cyprus, with different attractions for all ages. There is a large indoor play area for babies and toddlers and also child friendly rides outside, such as tea cups, choo-choo train or a trampoline. For others, there is a Ferris

23

wheel, and other family rides, but for the true daredevils, there is the most thrilling ride ever: Sling Shot!

Friendly tip: If you plan on staying for a shorter while, get tokens, but if you wish to spend a few hours there, or you are visiting with your family, buy a wristband.

15. SLING SHOT

This is the most popular attraction in Parko Paliatso, but only for the bravest. Sling Shot is a metal cage for two, hooked on steel cables where you are seated and securely strapped and then catapulted 80 meters into the air in just two seconds! There is a tiny camera inside the cage that captures every moment of your excitement and that DVD is given to you later as a gift. Price includes DVD, T-shirt and a life-long memory of the craziest thing you've done back in that summer when you visited Ayia Napa. Sling Shot is the bucket list must!

16. ZORBAS BAKERY

Zorbas bakery is the most popular bakery in the village. It is opened seven days a week, and it's located perfectly: just outside Luna park, or, on the way to Nissi beach, or, in the middle of bar area. It is perfect for every meal, from early breakfast to late night snack after bar crawling. It is offering a variety of Cypriot delicious pastries, coffees, sandwiches, pizzas or mouthwatering sweets and ice cream.

17. BEDROCK INN

Also a must! This great pub with the Flintstones themed décor, half naked and gorgeous bartenders, cocktails, shots and karaoke is simply calling your name. Yes, there is food, too. It is great for family snack during daytime, kids can take photos in Flintstones car, sing karaoke, but in the night the real party starts here. The latest attraction is the Silent Disco, where you can continue your party even when all the loud music has to be silenced (01 am).

18. AYIA THEKLA CHAPEL

A truly beautiful place. Don't know what other words to use. White arches and the blue roof are matching the Mediterranean scenery, disappearing in the blueness of the sea. This tiny rural church is a lovely landmark and one of the favorite spots for bridal photo sessions. There is a small cave just outside, where the Greek Orthodox Christians would hold liturgy (mass) in secret when Cyprus was under Turkish rule. Definitely worth a visit, and make sure it's during sunset, because of great scenery that will embellish your photos.

19. SING LIKE NOBODY IS LISTENING

Actually, everybody is listening, and very carefully, since the karaoke is one of the island's main entertainment forms. Everybody loves karaoke, old, young, kids, songbirds and whales. There are numerous pubs with karaoke animation teams that encourage undiscovered talents to sing. My choice is Tomy's pub. It is on excellent location, very large and

clean pub with great grill menu and fast service.
Happy hour is in plural, so grab a drink or two to
lubricate your vocal cords, pick a song and show the
crowd what you're made of.

20. VISIT PROTARAS

Ayia Napa's first neighbor, Protaras is an excellent
choice if you prefer family friendly and tranquil
holiday. Though it's also full of restaurants and pubs,
its' overall atmosphere is quieter. Where Ayia Napa
ends, Protaras begins, so go and explore. Visit some
stunning beaches like Fig Tree Bay, Konnos bay or
Green bay or simply stroll down the village, do some
trinket shopping, sit for a Frape and enjoy the view.
Protaras is famous for its Magic Dancing Waters
show, which has to be booked in advance and surely
not to be missed. Ghost town Famagusta is easily
reachable from Protaras.

21. MAGIC DANCING
WATERS

This is the most famous event in Protaras and has
to be booked in advance. The unforgettable and

spectacular show that combines music, water, lasers, lava, fire and smoke promises a night to remember. There is a buffet dinner available, but note that it is not included in the ticket price. The water and lights are dancing to classical and popular soundtracks for one hour. Needless to say that this experience will leave you amazed and another layer of satisfaction surely will be added for choosing the right holiday destination.

22. KONNOS BAY

Konnos Bay is located at the very edge of Ayia Napa where Protaras begins. This gorgeous bay is pine fringed and has sparkling, crystal clear azure waters. It is a very popular beach for locals and is rather well hidden so it makes a great little hideaway to head to for a change from the main touristic areas. This beach is absolutely perfect for children, as there are no waves. Sand is powdery soft, pine trees are sheltering you, water is warm and clear. Admire the sunset, (again me with this sunset thing, it can also be a sunrise if you prefer) and look for the starfish and some shells in the water. What else could you wish for?

23. FIG TREE BAY

As the name said – figs, everywhere and for free! Fig tree bay is also located in Protaras, but don't be discouraged, there is a local bus that circles from Ayia Napa to Paralimni village (Protaras is in the middle), and reaches other end in about 30 minutes, so for Protaras it takes like 15 minutes. The beach is very popular among families with small children, as for the very shallow waters. There is a small islet easily reachable by swimming. It is covered in low grass and it's completely inhabited. Fig Tree bay is another picturesque beach that you will love.

24. LOS BANDIDOS

Mexican food never tasted better on non-Mexican soil. Oh, and what a food! Los Bandidos is the place often booked for two weeks in advance. Start your evening with a pitcher of frozen Strawberry Margarita and choose a unique and yummy dish that will make you come back every time you're in Cyprus, or simply choose a bite from everything in the well-known form of Tapas. Whatever your choice would be, I am sure that visiting this place will be a smart choice when it comes to exploring food in Ayia Napa restaurants.

25. PLAY TAVLI

A board game for two players that is widely popular for many generations in Cyprus. In every Kafeneio, tavern or a betting shop, you can see a couple of seniors rolling dices, sometimes swearing, and even throwing checkers away in anger. Tavli is a bit complicated, and very addictive game whose object is to move all the checkers into your own home board and then bear them off. The first player to bear off all of their checkers is the winner. If you recognize the rules of the game – yes, you are right, it's Backgammon!

26. CYPRUS MEZE

The best possible way to get acquainted with Cypriot cuisine is to order a meze in Meze Restaurant (mezedopoleío). Meze is usually for two or more persons and it consists of 15-30 different appetizers (orektiko). They are never the same and restaurants mostly serve what they have fresh for that day. You

can always choose between typical Cyprus meze
(consists mostly of meat based dishes with only 2 or 3
fish plates) and fish meze (that is so delicious and
awesome, incredible choice of fish and seafood,
possibly 1 or 3 meat dishes in case there is not much
fresh fish in the restaurant at that moment). It is an
endless list of dishes, but I suggest these, to make
your mouth water: Tzatziki, Grilled Halloumi,
Lountza, Taramosalata, Stifado, Kleftiko, Koupes,
Lavraki, Grilled Octopus, and always leave room for
deserts. Try some Mahalepi, Rizogalo, Glyko Tou
Koutaliou (Spoon sweets), Pastelaki...

I'm so hungry now, be right back!

27. BRANDY SOUR

Brandy sour is The Cocktail.

It is the unofficial cocktail of Cyprus, as the recipe
originates from this island. While there are many
versions around the world, the Cypriot variety is a
distinct mixture, with absolutely and undoubtable
unique taste.

Take a little of the island home by using this easy
but secret recipe, not forgetting a bottle of cheap
Cyprus brandy (KEO) at the airport on the way home.

31

The secret recipe:

2 parts Cyprus brandy

1 part lemon juice

2-3 drops Angostura bitters (don't buy cheap substitutes)

Soda water or lemonade to fill

Directions:

Fill Highball glass with ice cubes

Add bitters, lemon juice and brandy

Fill with soda

Stir and garnish with a slice of fresh lemon

Serve immediately

Sip it slowly and enjoy the unique fresh, sweet and sour taste.

28. UV PAINT PARTY

Paint parties are known in Ayia Napa for years, but now, glowing paint is the hottest trend. These parties used to take place once a week in only one club, but now there are several clubs hosting the event, and the only difference makes the resident DJ and music of his choice (progressive, trending MTV hits, etc). Just imagine canons and guns filled with paint blasting at you from every corner of the club!

It's the ultimate party of the week and a holiday clubbing experience not to be missed.

29. FAMOUS LOCAL SPIRITS

Two spirits that are essential in Cyprus are Commandaria and Zivania.

Richard the Lionheart once proclaimed Commandaria to be the "Wine of Kings and King of Wines" It is the sweet dessert wine, and not just any wine: it is the world's oldest wine still in production, dating all the way back to 800 BC! It is made of autochthonous Cyprus red grapes and enjoyed as after-meal wine (like port), goes well with strong cheese and fresh fruit.

Zivania is only for the bold ones. It is well known local spirit, pomace brandy (in Cypriot, word zivana means pomace, and Zivania is derived from it). It contains very high level of alcohol. Cypriots keep their stash of Zivania in freezers and consume it ice cold, with some small appetizers (nuts, olives, ham or sausage bites). If a Cypriot welcomes you to his house, surely he will treat you with Zivania (possibly aged and preserved), as it is highly valued. Aged spirit will keep your tongue and belly burned for several days, so drink carefully and responsibly.

30. HALLOUMI

This is island's signature cheese that you have to try. It dates back to Medieval Byzantine period, and, usually in the past, batches of Halloumi were made by joint forces of an entire village. Nowadays, Halloumi is sold in every supermarket worldwide, but every small family restaurant has his own recipe, because it is an essential part of Cypriot's heritage. The white cheese is made of sheep and goat milk with traces of mint inside. It is best when grilled or fried. Give it a try, and I'm sure you'll bring it home as a perfect holiday souvenir.

31. ESCAPE ROOMS EXPERIENCE

Everywhere in the decent world, you have variety of Escape Rooms themes to choose from and have some fun with your crew. Ayia Napa is offering an excellent way to sober up a person with an unique type of remedy: Horror Maze and Paranoia Haunted

House! The moment you enter and start moving in the dark, pray not to wet your pants and embarrass yourself in front of your buddies. May the sobriety be with you!

32. TIE THE KNOT!

Ayia Napa, especially Nissi beach is known for their dream-come-true weddings. Organization is amazing, everything is adjusted to your taste, there are several wedding teams in Ayia Napa, and many hotels have their own wedding crews. This job is taken very seriously and you cannot imagine the possibilities. Just pick a spot, choose theme and food, don't forget rings and say the magic words!

33. GHOST TOWN FAMAGUSTA

Cyprus is a country divided. Ghost Town Famagusta is abandoned area of Northern Cyprus easily reachable from Ayia Napa, and the most popular way to explore it is to hop on the Open Top Red Bus that is operating three times a week. The ancient city of Famagusta is a remarkable site. The city is dotted with ruins, relics and interesting architecture. You will be taken to a once breathtaking Constantia beach, a touristic hotspot, now turned into a sad pile of sand where time stopped in 1974. Hear the story of Famagusta and walk among the ruins. Surely you will return as a changed person.

34. KAMARA TOU KORAKA

Stunningly beautiful natural bridge Kamara Tou Koraka is the most famous attraction in Cape Greko. This miracle of nature must be on your sightseeing list, especially if you know that it can collapse in the sea in every moment. The sea erosion of the stone and unfriendly and thick vegetation lead the bridge to the unsecure future. Visit it while it's still there!

35. WALKING TOUR

This is the best, the cheapest and the healthiest way to get to know the place you just arrived to. All Cypriots speak several foreign languages; many of them are native English or Russian speakers, so you will be guided properly but, I have to admit, there is a certain charm in listening to a native Cypriot while speaking English.

There are different kinds of walking tours; each is unique and incredibly interesting:

- Exploring the village and beaches tour
- Food tasting tour
- Bar crawling

The variety of choices in Ayia Napa will leave you speechless, but it will also burn a hole in your pocket. From mesmerizing beaches, fantastic souvenirs, local arts and crafts, different clubs and discos, incredible food choice, great wines and themed pubs for different crowd: pick your tour and don't forget to put the sunscreen on and grab that camera.

36. EXPLORE THE VILLAGE ON WHEELS

For those who prefer using steering wheel instead of feet, there are exciting options for getting familiar with the village and its surroundings. Quad bike safari is a well-known and long operated tour. Exploring the coastline using off road vehicles is lots of fun and a great adventure. Jeep safari is also a good alternative if you prefer a vehicle with chassis and a roof.

Tanja Andric

Driving around the neighborhood with skilled driver or expanding the tour around the whole island, there is no limit. There are so many hidden paths, small unknown beaches, churches, and diners for locals, disguised gems that are not on any official tourist map or guide. If none of this is your cup of tea, there is always a bike or segway rental to cruise around slowly and safely.

Take your time and make your own journey of discovery. Is the camera on?

37. RIVER REGGAE PUB

If you are looking for a place to chill after a hard party night, River Reggae Pub is the right place to be. This is one of Ayia Napa's longest running clubs and is an essential part of any clubber's holiday. With its exotic environment, large swimming pool, dance floor and cozy booths, excellent open air bars (and hot bartenders) it proves to be an outstanding venue and a definite must do on your checklist.

38. SHIPWRECK DIVING

This is an absolute diving experience and I highly recommend it to everybody, not just professional divers. There are three local wrecks and the world famous Zenobia wreck in Larnaka district. Plunge in with professionals, hear some interesting stories and see boats that now serve as artificial reefs and marine reserve. Get face to face with Eels, Barracudas and Groupers and make sure you have a camera with you.

39. FINE DINING

Between bar crawling, exploring village's fast food and local cuisine scene, let yourself be surprised by some serious fine dining right in the heart of the busy Square. There are several restaurants with very formal atmosphere and menus for upscale clientele. In my opinion, Sage, Glasshouse Lounge and UMI Sushi bar are places definitely worth visiting.

40. FRAPPE

Frappe, is a foam-covered iced coffee drink made from instant coffee. It is the default order at any local cafe, especially in the summer. One or two teaspoons of instant coffee (traditionally Nescafe), sugar (or without any) and a little water are blended to form a foam, which is then poured into a tall glass with an obligatory straw. There are many options regarding taste, and here is the quick guide.

Sketo (Plain) – 2 tsp coffee, no sugar
Metrio (Medium) – 2 tsp coffee, 1-2 tsp sugar
Glyko (Sweet) – 2 tsp coffee, 4 tsp sugar
Mavro (Black) – 100% water
Ligo Gala (A bit of milk) – Add just a little bit of milk
Miso-Miso (Half-Half) – 50% water, 50% milk
Olo Gala (All Milk) – 100% milk

Seems confusing, but after tasting two or three options (Metrio Miso-Miso, or Sketo Mavro, or Glyko Ligo Gala, etc), you will easily learn which combination is perfect to your taste.

41. I LOVE AYIA NAPA MONUMENT

Honestly, I don't know a single person who's been to Ayia Napa and doesn't have a photo there. You love the Square, you certainly love all the bars and nightlife of the Square, you surely love mesmerizing colors and clarity of beaches, so, you do love Ayia Napa, and the monument is an ode to that statement!

42. DEEP SEA FISHING TRIP

This is a very cool and adventurous excursion, one of my favorites. Deep sea fishing trip offers you a chance to catch Tuna, Swordfish, or any other local fish and do something different. You will spend the whole day on the boat with professionals who will help you catch the big one. There is nothing like watching the sunrise over the Mediterranean, as you enjoy a tasty breakfast on board. Word of caution: there are no dolphins in the area, so don't go for false promises.

43. BLACK AND WHITE CLUB

If you love RnB, Hip-Hop, Dancehall or Reggae this is the place to be. The club itself is not really big, it gets crowded quickly so you can dance back to back with strangers and feel the vibe. People really love this club, its innovative look and hot atmosphere.

44. CARWASH

If your ears hurt from constant heavy beat of today's hit music, you need a remedy, asap; Carwash disco is what doctor ordered! 70's, 80's 90's dance hits, take off your high heels and dance the night away! Go crazy, wear a polyester neon colored wig and sing along:

"At the car wash, woooh

Talking about the car wash, yeah

Come on y'all and sing it for me

Car wash, woooh, car wash yeah" – Rose Royce, Carwash

45. CASTLE CLUB

Castle club is the ultimate clubbing experience on the island, probably one of the best in Europe, not sure about the world. It is huge, gigantic and majestic. It will devour you the moment you innocently set your foot in. Choose between five different arenas, all underground, or chill in VIP lounge. Whatever your choice will be, surely the Castle club will remain pinned on the top of your clubbing list.

46. PANCYPRIAN WATERMELON FESTIVAL

Watermelon Festival is such a wonderful occasion to visit village of Frenaros, just a few minutes away by car or bus from Ayia Napa. The celebration dedicated to this yummy fruit is taking place on July 16th and you can enjoy in good music of local artists, dances, children are also involved in numerous activities, and everybody is having great time. One of the festival highlights is having a scoop of watermelon ice cream, drinking a watermelon based cocktails, or simply taking a fresh one home.

43

47. AYIA NAPA FESTIVAL

Ayia Napa festival is an excellent opportunity to mingle with the locals, feel the language, see the variety of folk dances, maybe some readings or plays done in different Cypriot dialects, taste the local dishes and enjoy in concerts of big local stars and some international guests. The best about this festival: entrance is free!

48. STROLL DOWN LIMANAKI

Small but beautiful harbor of Ayia Napa is the ideal place for an evening walk. Taste local food in many excellent fish and traditional food restaurants while listening to traditional Greek Cypriot music, do the trinket shopping, or simply take your darling by the hand and sit by the lighthouse and watch the sun go down. There are cats. Many cats, everywhere. Bring them some dinner leftovers.

49. VISIT KAFENEIO

Kafeneio (coffee shop) is a traditional and rustic small place where mustached old men sit and have a cup of local coffee (Cypriot coffee – grounded coffee beans soaked in boiling water, leaving a residue on the bottom of the very small mug. Takes a bit of skill and patience to prepare this type of coffee, but it is a delicious alternative to Espresso and you simply have to taste it). Go there, sit on those old squeaky chairs and try your Tavli skills.

50. MAKE A PROMISE

Now with your vacation officially finished, what else is there to be done? Summarize your impressions, pack your bags and go to Zorbas bakery for the last frape and haloumi pie and some takeaway sweets. Kiss Nissi beach good-bye, and when exiting Ayia Napa to get on the highway to the Larnaka airport, look back to Makronissos and make a promise to come back next year!

BONUS TIPS:

So far mentioned, fifty tips, represented the official part of this guidebook, and they are mostly focused on summer. I would also like to explain, what are Christmas and Easter celebrations like, and maybe with a few personal advices, tease you enough to decide to visit the village during these two holidays. Cyprus can offer to the visitors so much more to discover without tight connections to summer holidays

You should know that Cyprus is country with 300 days of sunshine, so it's practically summer all year round, but the temperature and humidity is not equal in May and December.

The summer season ends in final weeks of October and after that, majority of clubs, pubs and other venues closes for the winter renovations, and you might be unpleasantly surprised how that vibrant village of Ayia Napa turned into Ghost town overnight. This is really important to know, because people keep flocking to the village, attracted by very cheap flight and accommodation prices, and then get disappointed.

Cypriots celebrate Christmas on December 25th and the festive season is officially opened by all day events on the first Sunday in December on Ayia Napa Square, spreading Christmas vibes all across the village.

Lighting the Christmas tree is the crescendo of the joyous countdown period to Christmas Eve. Police Orchestra along with other music groups start playing Christmas music and songs, there are stands with lots of wine and later with fireworks in the sky. During daytime Charity Flea market is organized and I cannot describe what treasures can be found on such markets. From preloved clothes, toys and books, to some rare souvenirs, stamps, books and framed photos, some even date from past centuries. I really love digging through boxes in flea markets, but knowing that every Euro spent is for charity, gives the special flavor to this event.

Another pre-Christmas event that is regularly taking place is the inaugural Ayia Napa Marathon. The best part of the marathon is the so called "Fun Run", where people have the opportunity to run or walk in festive costumes and contribute to charity which is the main cause of this part of the event. Usual December temperature goes between 17 and 19 degrees Celsius (62-66°F), so it's really perfect for such outdoor activity.

Tanja Andric

After Christmas celebration, which is different every year in artists and performances around the village, comes the celebration of New Year, and I really haven't got enough words to describe the joy in the air (read: alcoholic vapors), the happiness, people dancing on the Square to the music of several DJ's, Santa giving gifts to kids, dance performances, traditional food is served, and all wrapped up with breathtaking fireworks! The biggest Ayia Napa clubs open for this occasion, and many restaurants and hotels offer special dinners and special menus.

Just after you sobered up and thought about what else to do, church bells will toll, inviting all of you to gather in Ayia Napa harbor to celebrate Epiphany and swim for the Holy Cross in icy waters. Epiphany takes place on January 6th and comes from the Greek word meaning "To reveal", as it is when the baby Jesus was "revealed" to the world. On the eve of Epiphany, the feast day is heralded by children singing carols (kalanta). They take the message of Jesus' baptism in the Jordan River from house to house. On the next day, the service of the Great Sanctification of Water is held. Then, in Ayia Napa Harbor a ceremony is held to bless the water and the blessing is confirmed when the priest casts a cross into the water and a dove that symbolizes the Holy

Spirit is released. Fierce young men dive into the water to retrieve the cross, and the individual who recovers it and returns it to the priest is given a cross as a gift and receives a special blessing, believed to provide greater luck for the year ahead.

This is so much better than Ice Bucket Challenge. Epiphany is a real men challenge. Needless to say that diving for the cross is the bucket list must!

Important to know: During December, majority of pubs and restaurants that are opened are located on the Square, or very close to it. If you still don't like that much peace and quiet around Ayia Napa, rent a car and visit nearby Larnaka and the charming Finikoudes promenade, or, head to the capital, Nicosia, where everything is vibrant and vivid, round the clock.

Another grand celebration deserves to be described in this book, because you never know when will your suitcase call, and announce that it's time to pack for Cyprus.

Easter (Pasha) is the most important religious celebration in the Greek Christian Orthodox Church. It is a joyous time of year and a wonderful period to be on the island. The sun is shining, but evenings are cold with chances of rain.

After forty days of fasting, as Easter Sunday is approaching, you can see people happy people around the village, preparing for the big celebration.

The gathering points in the final days before Easter are churches (Ayia Napa monastery, Ayia Thekla chapel) and homes where hardworking housewives start baking flaounes (short crust with cheese, eggs, raisings and mint filling – very yummy) and dying hard boiled eggs in red (symbolizing Christ's Blood from the Cross). The crucifixion of Christ is on Thursday, so in the evening, people go to church to "mourn". All the icons are covered with black veils to show their grief.

On the Good Friday (or "Great Friday" in Greek) families carrying flowers, gather in all the churches around the island (In Ayia Napa, follow the crowd to the Monastery). The flowers are collected and carried by young girls to decorate the "Epitaphios" (the icon which depicts Christ after being removed from the cross) during the church service. In the evening, young men carry the "Epitaphios" outside the church around the area and back to the church, with people following it the whole time. Since the Friday is still "mourning" period, this process might give you creepy chills down your spine.

Easter Saturday is a final countdown to Easter Sunday. At 11 pm, the Service of Resurrection is held; church bells are loudly tolling, inviting everyone to join the celebration of the resurrection of Jesus Christ. Huge bonfires are lit and everybody carries a large unlit candle (lambada). During the midnight service, candles are lit by the Holy Light (brought straight from Jerusalem) and many people take home their candle for blessing. Please note that not a single bar or a restaurant is opened til 01am. After the midnight service there is a long expected feast. People eat a special kind of soup Avgolemono (lemon-egg chicken soup). They also crack the red eggs and say "Christos Anesti" which means "Christ has risen," and your response should be "Alithos Anesti" which means "Indeed He has risen".

Easter Sunday is when the celebrations really begin. Feasts of souvla (large pieces of lamb or pork, or chicken are cooked on an open charcoal fire), salads, sweets, and alcohol, rivers of alcohol! Easter lunch is so worth of 40 days fasting! The smell of outdoor barbeques infuses the whole island! Get prepared for the whole day and night of different programmes on the Square. From national dances,

Tanja Andric

Greek music concerts and poetry reading, to some traditional games (bag racing, egg on spoon, etc)

You don't have to be a believer, the festive atmosphere will spread through your body and you will find yourself eating tones of souvla, drinking Zivania, cracking red eggs and saying "Kalo Pasha" (Happy Easter)!

TOP REASONS TO BOOK THIS TRIP

Beaches: The beaches here are often compared to Caribbean, so, no need to go halfway around the globe to enjoy white sand and warm crystal clear water. From cliffs and rocks to powdery sand, it is a huge variety of beaches. Some are wide and long, others are remote and hidden, but exploring as much beaches as your holiday schedule lets you, can be a perfect introduction into planning on returning next year, because you haven't visited them all.

Food: The food represents a fantastic variety of flavors, amazing mix of Greek and Turkish spices and dishes, also with a scent of Byzantium and Middle Eastern cuisines. You cannot find one excellent dish; there are dozens, from starters to desserts, so don't stick to the known international fast food franchises, go explore tastes and I am sure you will find so much more delicacies that suit your personal eating habits.

Island Culture: I am trying to put it all in one small paragraph, but it's impossible. The whole island is bursting with culture, rich heritage and tradition.

Tanja Andric

Ayia Napa was inhabited from prehistorical period and represents unique mixture of different civilizational influences because it is located on the crossroads of Europe and Middle East. Apart from wild nightlife you can feed your crave for art. Not to mention that only 25 kilometers east from Ayia Napa, the fascinating Famagusta (Othello) castle is overlooking the Mediterranean and Richard Lionheart's Castle (Kolossi) is set in town of Limassol. Famagusta (Othello) castle got its name from Shakespeare's famous play Othello, which is set in a harbor town in Cyprus.

Cyprus is a vibrant land full of differences; it does not let you stay indifferent. This is the only country in the world that has a divided capital. Try to imagine yourself walking down your capital city and suddenly, there is a wall, splitting it in two pieces, belonging to two different countries. This is life in Cyprus from 1974, Greek and Turkish Cypriots have learned how to coexist during past decades, and it is very interesting to see the influences from both sides overflowing.

Bonus Book

50 THINGS TO KNOW ABOUT PACKING LIGHT FOR TRAVEL

Pack the Right Way Every Time

Author: Manidipa Bhattacharyya

Tanja Andric

Edited by Melanie Howthorne

Introduction

He who would travel happily
must travel light.

-Antoine de Saint-Exupéry

Travel takes you to different places from seas and mountains to deserts and much more. In your travels you get to interact with different people and their cultures. You will, however, enjoy the sights and interact positively with these new people even more, if you are travelling light.

When you travel light your mind can be free from worry about your belongings. You do not have to spend precious vacation time waiting for your luggage to arrive after a long flight. There is be no chance of your bags going missing and the best part is that you need not pay a fee for checked baggage.

People who have mastered this art of packing light will root for you to take only one carry-on, wherever you go. However, many people can find it really hard to pack light. More so if you are travelling with children. Differentiating between "must have" and "just in case" items is the starting point. There will be ample shopping avenues at your destination which are just waiting to be explored.

Tanja Andric

This book will show you 'packing' in a new 'light' –
pun intended – and help you to embrace light
packing practices for all of your future travels.

Off to packing!

Dedication

I dedicate this book to all the travel buffs that I know,
who have given me great insights into the contents of
their backpacks.

About The Author

Manidipa Bhattacharyya is a creative writer and editor, with an education in English literature and Linguistics. After working in the IT industry for seven long years she decided to call it quits and follow her heart instead. Manidipa has been ghost writing, editing, proof reading and doing secondary research services for many story tellers and article writers for about three years. She stays in Kolkata, India with her husband and a busy two year old. In her own time Manidipa enjoys travelling, photography and writing flash fiction.

Manidipa believes in travelling light and never carries anything that she couldn't haul herself on a trip. However, travelling with her child changed the scenario. She seemed to carry the entire world with her for the baby on the first two trips. But good sense prevailed and she is again working her way to becoming a light traveler, this time with a kid.

Tanja Andric

The Right Travel Gear

1. Choose Your Travel Gear Carefully

While selecting your travel gear, pick items that are light weight, durable and most importantly, easy to carry. There are cases with wheels so you can drag them along – these are usually on the heavy side because of the trolley. Alternatively a backpack that you can carry comfortably on your back, or even a duffel bag that you can carry easily by hand or sling across your body are also great options. Whatever you choose, one thing to keep in mind is that the luggage itself should not weigh a ton, this will give you the flexibility to bring along one extra pair of shoes if you so desire.

2. Carry The Minimum Number Of Bags

Selecting light weight luggage is not everything. You need to restrict the number of bags you carry as well. One carry-on size bag is ideal for light travel. Most carriers allow one cabin baggage plus one purse, handbag or camera bag as long as it slides under the seat in front. So technically, you can carry two items of luggage without checking them in.

3. Pack One Extra Bag

Always pack one extra empty bag along with your essential items. This could be a very light weight duffel bag or even a sturdy tote bag which takes up minimal space. In the event that you end up buying a lot of souvenirs, you already have a handy bag to stuff all that into and do not have to spend time hunting for an appropriate bag.

I'm very strict with my packing and have everything in its right place. I never change a rule. I hardly use anything in the hotel room. I wheel my own wardrobe in and that's it.

Charlie Watts

Clothes & Accessories

4. Plan Ahead

Figure out in advance what you plan to do on your trip. That will help you to pick that one dress you need for the occasion. If you are going to attend a wedding then you have to carry formal wear. If not, you can ditch the gown for something lighter that will be comfortable during long walks or on the beach.

5. Wear That Jacket

Remember that wearing items will not add extra luggage for your air travel. So wear that bulky jacket that you plan to carry for your trip. This saves space and can also help keep you warm during the chilly flight.

6. Mix and Match

Carry clothes that can be interchangeably used to reinvent your look. Find one top that goes well with a couple of pairs of pants or skirts. Use tops, shirts and jackets wisely along with other accessories like a scarf or a stole to create a new look.

7. Choose Your Fabric Wisely

Stuffing clothes in cramped bags definitely takes its toll which results in wrinkles. It is best to carry wrinkle free, synthetic clothes or merino tops. This will eliminate the need for that small iron you usually bring along.

8. Ditch Clothes Pack Underwear

Pack more underwear and socks. These are the things that will give you a fresh feel even if you do not get a chance to wear fresh clothes. Moreover these are easy to wash and can be dried inside the hotel room itself.

9. Choose Dark Over Light

While picking your clothes choose dark coloured ones. They are easy to colour coordinate and can last longer before needing a wash. Accidental food spills and dirt from the road are less visible on darker clothes.

10. Wear Your Jeans

Take only one pair of Jeans with you, which you should wear on the flight. Remember to pick a pair that can be worn for sightseeing trips and is equally eloquent for dinner. You can add variety by adding light weight cargoes and chinos.

11. Carry Smart Accessories

The right accessory can give you a fresh look even with the same old dress. An intelligent neck-piece, a couple of bright scarves, stoles or a sarong can be used in a number of ways to add variety to your clothing. These light weight beauties can double up as a nursing cover, a light blanket, beach wear, a modesty cover for visiting places of worship, and also makes for an enthralling game of peek-a-boo.

12. Learn To Fold Your Garments

Seasoned travellers all swear by rolling their clothes for compact and wrinkle free packing. Bundle packing, where you roll the clothes around a central object as if tying it up, is also a popular method of compact and wrinkle free packing. Stacking folded clothes one on top of another is a big no-no as it makes creases extreme and they are difficult to get rid of without ironing.

13. Wash Your Dirty Laundry

One of the ways to avoid carrying loads of clothes is to wash the clothes you carry. At some places you might get to use the laundry services or a Laundromat but if you are in a pinch, best solution is to wash them yourself. If that is the plan then carrying quick drying clothes is highly recommended, which most often also happen to be the wrinkle free variety.

14. Leave Those Towels Behind

Regular towels take up a lot of space, are heavy and take ages to dry out. If you are staying at hotels they will provide you with towels anyway. If you are travelling to a remote place, where the availability of towels look doubtful, carry a light weight travel towel of viscose material to do the job.

15. Use A Compression Bag

Compression bags are getting lots of recommendation now days from regular travellers. These are useful for saving space in your luggage when you have to pack bulky dresses. While packing for the return trip, get help from the hotel staff to arrange a vacuum cleaner.

Footwear

16. Put On Your Hiking Boots

If you have plans to go hiking or trekking during your trip, you will need those bulky hiking boots. The best way to carry them is to wear them on flight to save space and luggage weight. You can remove the boots once inside and be comfortable in your socks.

17. Picking The Right Shoes

Shoes are often the bulkiest items, along with being the dainty if you are a female. They need care and take up a lot of space in your luggage. It is advisable therefore to pick shoes very carefully. If you plan to do a lot of walking and site seeing, then wearing a pair of comfortable walking shoes are a must. For more formal occasions you can carry durable, light weight flats which will not take up much space.

18. Stuff Shoes

If you happen to pack a pair of shoes, ensure you utilize their hollow insides. Tuck small items like rolled up socks or belts to save space. They will also be easy to find.

Toiletries
19. Stashing Toiletries

Carry only absolute necessities. Airline rules dictate that for one carry-on bag, liquids and gels must be in 3.4 ounce (100ml) bottles or less, and must be packed in a one quart zip-lock bag. If you are planning to stay in a hotel, the basic things will be provided for you. It's best is to buy the rest from the local market at your destination.

20. Take Along Tampons

Tampons are a hard to find item in a lot of countries. Figure out how many you need and pack accordingly. For longer stays you can buy them online and have them delivered to where you are staying.

21. Get Pampered Before You Travel

Some avid travellers suggest getting a pedicure and manicure just the day before travelling. This not only gives you a well kept look, you also save the trouble of packing nail polish. Remember, every little bit of weight reduced adds up.

Electronics
22. Lugging Along Electronics

Electronics have a large role to play in our lives today. Most of us cannot imagine our lives away from our phones, laptops or tablets. However while travelling, one must consider the amount of weight these electronics add to our luggage. Thankfully smart phones come along with all the essentials tools like a camera, email access, picture editing tools and more. They are smart to the point of eliminating the need to carry multiple gadgets. Choose a smart phone that suits all your requirements and travel with the world in your palms or pocket.

23. Reduce the Number of Chargers

If you do travel with multiple electronic devices, you will have to bear the additional burden of carrying all their chargers too. Check if a single charger can be used for multiple devices. You might also consider investing in a pocket charger. These small devices support multiple devices while keeping you charged on the go.

24. Travel Friendly Apps

Along with smart phones come numerous apps, which are immensely helpful in our travels. You name it and you have an app for it at hand – take pictures, sharing with friends and family, torch to light dark roads, maps, checking flight/train times, find hotels and many other things. Use these smart alternatives to traditional items like books to eliminate weight and save space.

I get ideas about what's essential when packing my suitcase.

-Diane von Furstenberg

Travelling With Kids

25. Bring Along the Stroller

Kids might enjoy walking for a while but they soon tire out and a stroller is the just the right thing for them to rest in while you continue your tour. Strollers also double duty as a luggage carrier and shopping bag holder. Remember to pick a light weight, easy to handle brand of stroller. Better yet, find out in advance if you can rent a stroller at your destination.

26. Bring Only Enough Diapers for Your Trip

Diapers take up a lot of space and add to the weight of your luggage. Therefore it is advisable to carry just enough diapers to last through the trip and a few for afterwards, till you buy fresh stock at your destination. Unless of course you are travelling to a really remote area, in which case you have no choice but to carry the load. Otherwise diapers are something you will find pretty easily.

27. Take Only A Couple Of Toys

Children are easily attracted by new things in their environment. While travelling they will find numerous 'new' objects to scrutinize and play with. Packing just one favorite toy is enough, or if there is no favorite toy leave out all of them in favor of stories or imaginary games.

28. Carry Kid Friendly Snacks

Create a small snack counter in your bag to store away quick bites for those sudden hunger pangs. Depending on the child's age this could include chocolates, raisins, dry fruits, granola bars or biscuits. Also keep a bottle of water handy for your little one. These things do not add much weight and can be adjusted in a handbag or knapsack.

29. Games to Carry

Create some travel specific, imaginary games if you have slightly grown up children, like spot the attractions. Keep a coloring book and colors handy for in-flight or hotel time. Apps on your smart phone can keep the children engaged with cartoons and story books. Older children are often entertained by games available on phones or tablets. This cuts the weight of luggage down while keeping the kids entertained.

30. Let the Kids Carry Their Load

A good thing is to start early sharing of responsibilities. Let your child pick a bag of his or her choice and pack it themselves. Keep tabs on what they are stuffing in their bags by asking if they will be using that item on the trip. It could start out being just an entertainment bag initially but with growing years they will learn to sort the useful from the superfluous. Children as little as four can maneuver a small trolley suitcase like a pro- their experience in pull along toys credit. If you are worried that you may be pulling it for them, you may want to start with a backpack.

31. Decide on Location for Children to Sleep

While on a trip you might not always get a crib at your destination, and carrying one will make life all the more difficult. Instead call ahead to see if there are any cribs or roll out beds for children. You may even put blankets on the floor. Weave them a story about camping and they will gladly sleep without any trouble.

32. Get Baby Products Delivered At Your Destination

If you are absolutely paranoid about not getting your favourite variety of diaper or brand of baby food, check out online stores like amazon.com for services in your destination city. You can buy things online ahead of your travel and get them delivered to your hotel upon arrival.

33. Feeding Needs Of Your Infants

If you are travelling with a breastfed infant, you save the trouble of carrying bottles and bottle sanitization kits. For special food, or medications, you may need to call ahead to make sure you have a refrigerator where you are staying.

34. Feeding Needs of Your Toddler

With the progression from infancy to toddler, their dietary requirements too evolve. You will have to pack some snacks for travelling time. Fresh fruits and vegetables can be purchased at your destination. Most of the cities you travel to in whichever part of the world, will have baby food products and formulas, available at the local drug-store or the supermarket.

35. Picking Clothes for Your Baby

Contrary to popular belief, babies can do without many changes of clothes. At the most pack 2 outfits per day. Pack mix and match type clothes for your little one as well. Pick things which are comfortable to wear and quick to dry.

36. Selecting Shoes for Your Baby

Like outfits, kids can make do with two pairs of comfortable shoes. If you can get some water resistant shoes it will be best. To expedite drying wet shoes, you can stuff newspaper in them then wrap them with newspaper and leave them to dry overnight.

37. Keep One Change of Clothes Handy

Travelling with kids can be tricky. Keep a change of clothes for the kids and mum handy in your purse or tote bag. This takes a bit of space in your hand luggage but comes extremely handy in case there are any accidents or spills.

38. Leave Behind Baby Accessories

Baby accessories like their bed, bath tub, car seat, crib etc. should be left at home. Many hotels provide a crib on request, while car seats can be borrowed from friends or rented. Babies can be given a bath in the hotel sink or even in the adult bath tub with a little bit of water. If you bring a few bath toys, they can be used in the bath, pool, and out of water. They can also be sanitized easily in the sink.

39. Carry a Small Load Of Plastic Bags

With children around there are chances of a number of soiled clothes and diapers. These plastic bags help to sort the dirt from the clean inside your big bag. These are very light weight and come in handy to other carry stuff as well at times.

Pack with a Purpose

40. Packing for Business Trips

One neutral-colored suit should suffice. It can be paired with different shirts, ties and accessories for different occasions. One pair of black suit pants could be worn with a matching jacket for the office or with a snazzy top for dinner.

41. Packing for A Cruise

Most cruises have formal dinners, and that formal dress usually takes up a lot of space. However you might find a tuxedo to rent. For women, a short black dress with multiple accessory options will do the trick.

42. Packing for A Long Trip Over Different Climates

The secret packing mantra for travel over multiple climates is layering. Layering traps air around your body creating insulation against the cold. The same light t-shirt that is comfortable in a warmer climate can be the innermost layer in a colder climate.

Reduce Some More Weight

43. Leave Precious Things At Home

Things that you would hate to lose or get damaged leave them at home. Precious jewelry, expensive gadgets or dresses, could be anything. You will not

Tanja Andric

require these on your trip. Leave them at home and
spare the load on your mind.

44. Send Souvenirs by Mail

If you have spent all your money on purchasing
souvenirs, carrying them back in the same bag that
you brought along would be difficult. Either pack
everything in another bag and check it in the airport
or get everything shipped to your home. Use an
international carrier for a secure transit, but this could
be more expensive than the checking fees at the
airport.

45. Avoid Carrying Books

Books equal to weight. There are many reading apps
which you can download on your smart phone or tab.
Plus there are gadgets like Kindle and Nook that are
thinner and lighter alternatives to your regular book.

Check, Get, Set, Check Again

46. Strategize Before Packing

Create a travel list and prepare all that you think you
need to carry along. Keep everything on your bed or
floor before packing and then think through once
again – do I really need that? Any item that meets this

question can be avoided. Remove whatever you don't really need and pack the rest.

47. Test Your Luggage

Once you have fully packed for the trip take a test trip with your luggage. Take your bags and go to town for window shopping for an hour. If you enjoy your hour long trip it is good to go, if not, go home and reduce the load some more. Repeat this test till you hit the right weight.

48. Add a Roll Of Duct Tape

You might wonder why, when this book has been talking about reducing stuff, we're suddenly asking you to pack something totally unusual. This is because when you have limited supplies, duct tape is immensely helpful for small repairs – a broken bag, leaking zip-lock bag, broken sunglasses, you name it and duct tape can fix it, temporarily.

49. List of Essential Items

Even though the emphasis is on packing light, there are things which have to be carried for any trip. Here is our list of essentials:

• Passport/Visa or any other ID

- Any other paper work that might be required on a trip like permits, hotel reservation confirmations etc.

- Medicines – all your prescription medicines and emergency kit, especially if you are travelling with children

- Medical or vaccination records

- Money in foreign currency if travelling to a different country

- Tickets- Email or Message them to your phone

50. Make the Most of Your Trip

Wherever you are going, whatever you hope to do we encourage you to embrace it whole-heartedly. Take in the scenery, the culture and above all, enjoy your time away from home.

On a long journey even a straw weighs heavy.

-Spanish Proverb

Packing and Planning Tips

A Week before Leaving

- Arrange for someone to take care of pets and water plants

- •Stop mail and newspaper

- Notify Credit Card companies where you are going.

- Change your thermostat settings

- Car inspected, oil is changed, and tires have the correct pressure.

- Passports and id is up to date.

- Pay bills.

- Copy important items and download travel Apps.

- Start collecting small bills for tips

Right Before Leaving

- Clean out refrigerator.

- Empty garbage cans.

- Lock windows.

- Make sure you have the right ID with you.

- Bring cash for tips.

- Remember travel documents.

- Lock door behind you.

- Remember wallet.

- Unplug items in house and pack chargers.

Tanja Andric

Read other Greater Than a Tourist Books

Tanja Andric

> TOURIST

Visit Greater Than a Tourist for Free Travel Tips
http://GreaterThanATourist.com

Sign up for the Greater Than a Tourist Newsletter for discount days, new books, and travel information:
http://eepurl.com/cxspyf

Follow us on Facebook for tips, images, and ideas:
https://www.facebook.com/GreaterThanATourist

Follow us on Pinterest for travel tips and ideas:
http://pinterest.com/GreaterThanATourist

Follow us on Instagram for beautiful travel images:
http://Instagram.com/GreaterThanATourist

Tanja Andric

> TOURIST

Please leave your honest review of this book on Amazon and Goodreads. Please send your feedback to GreaterThanaTourist@gmail.com as we continue to improve the series. Thank you. We appreciate your positive and constructive feedback. Thank you.

Tanja Andric

NOTES

Tanja Andric

Printed in Great Britain
by Amazon

29297429R00057